UNCOMMON LABELS

Fiona Hutchings

WRITTEN OFF
Publishing

First published in Great Britain by Written Off Publishing, 2024
Copyright © Fiona Hutchings, 2024
The moral right of the author has been asserted.

Written Off does not use AI.

Author photo © Ary Hutchings

ISBN: 978-1-915320-36-0

Written Off Publishing
Owley Wood Road
Weaverham
Cheshire
CW8 3LF

writtenoffpublishing.com

Edited by Rebecca Kenny @ Written Off
Cover art © Samantha Sanderson-Marshall @ SMASH Designs Books
smashdesigns.co.uk

Printed in the UK by Mixam Ltd.

For my favourite human beans. Always.

CONTENTS

INTRODUCTION

This poetry collection is based around the theme of labels.

We all have experience of being labelled — some we choose or identify ourselves; others are forced on us against our will, or are weaponised against us.

I have had labels attached to me from birth. I was born with a degenerative congenital bone disease called Osteogenesis Imperfecta (OI). It was explained to me when I was still young that the name translated as my bones being imperfect from the very start; my DNA was mutated — and that was before I was presented with the additional labels of 'female', 'Northern' and 'working class'.

These poems explore some of the labels — common and not — that have been given to me and my experience of embodying them. In exploring them together, we will make horrible dinner ladies nauseous, confuse medical students and even come out of the closet.

I hope you find something you can relate to.

UNCOMMON LABELS

WHY CAN'T I BE YOUR HERO

I can't be your hero
Though I am flattered you wanted me to be
The height of this pedestal is dizzying
You champion me to strangers
Hold me up as a model of resilience
I demure politely
And you always reply with variations on a theme
You say many others wouldn't have continued
The fact I have a job is worthy of praise
Getting back up over and over
No matter how many times life steamrollers
Splits, explodes, rends and rips it up
I start again and you cheer
What you mean is I'm not fulfilling the assumptions
The ones crowding your brain you refuse to see
You try to hide your relief that it's not you
And instead, perform the pity you perceive I must warrant
By lionising me
Listing my history like a litany
Counting miracles back to me
I don't dispute the miraculous comebacks against crippling odds
But you credit me with more powers than I have
My body simply carried on with no input from me
It takes every scan, scalpel and stitch
Because it doesn't know any other way.

A heroic identity must be earned, surely?

BEING MY CARER

I never wanted you to be my carer
Children far too tiny to be the bearer
Of a parent's life, an unbearable weight
Robbing you of the chance to create
And learn through chaos, fun and mess
Instead all focused on my progress
Being so young and yet so quiet
Never daring to start a childish riot
Such adult concerns resting on your shoulder
Juggling the anxieties of someone much older
The reality of death dropped on your head
Pale little faces trying to hide their dread
Waiting for the next thing to go catastrophically wrong
Thinking that for me you've got to be strong
While still learning to spell your own name
Also wondering if you're somehow to blame
Daily fears at home-time each day
That if I wasn't there I'd really gone away
That if you couldn't see me, I might have died
Then, fierce cuddles as on me you cried
Repeating that you're sorry for making me sad
If you made me ill that would be bad
Constantly checking if there was anything you could do
Agonising guilt at what I put you through
I never wanted you to be my carer
I'd done it too and wanted life to be fairer
For you to have a family where your needs were met
Instead of these traumas I know you can't forget
I know sometimes you feel overwhelmed
By a life that makes you feel compelled
To always factor in my needs before your own
Sometimes afraid to leave me alone
But you have also grown into your role
Accepted that somethings you can't control

Reshaped your trauma to help shape services
Making them more fit for the purpose of
Supporting other young carers like you
By sharing your experiences and different view
Talking to adults in powerful positions
Telling your own stories to politicians
Taking statistics and giving them a face
Politely, determinedly stating your case
Talking about the part of your life often hidden
And for so many other young people all across Britain

THE ALIENATED WOMAN

I decided to write an anthology for my dissertation
Because, I figured, that would be freer of needless complication
Mostly because I hated the dry, factual needs of university
I had really expected more in the way of diversity

I'd anticipated lots of scope to capture and create
Sights, sounds and words, have them marked first rate
Writing creatively I could do — even if I couldn't spell
But academic essays were a boring and special type of hell

I did try to focus, show willing, but attention was not my friend
The ones who did try to help me got driven round the bend
So the dissertation, I decided, would need to match my skills
Adding an accidental English minor added some extra frills

To my currently dull and dowdy-looking degree
Plus I figured this way it'd end up more a bit more... *me*
I started working on short stories, full of angst and song
Often getting distracted by the mixtape created as I went along

A woman in a club where the owner is actually the devil
Played a synth-punk soundtrack as Satan and his followers revel
Women harassed on the tube call male assailants rats
Some just desserts are then dispensed in their natural habitat

One woman runs decisions past a rock star on her wall
Freddie Mercury somehow never failed to answer her call
There were stories told on message apps and a funeral hit list
Women used, abandoned and dead that no one seemed to miss

People who read said they could see me in every story I wrote
I could see the flickers in the way a character might emote
Songs that were my favourites; rats were my biggest fear
But I was the writer, nothing else; wasn't my job to disappear?

My supervisor was a lovely woman, although a bit scatty
I seemed to do most of the talking, she was not really very chatty
As deadline loomed I couldn't tell if the book was OK or a bit shit
Neither did I have a concept, or theme, or title to put a label on it

She read the printouts slowly; I was nervous and wanted a smoke
Or a nap. A lie down. My eyes were heavy when she finally spoke:
'You've used your life and now to fruition comes your masterplan
For these are the various tales of you, The Alienated Woman'

PEOPLE ARE LIKE BIRDS

People are like beady-eyed birds
They peck at you endlessly with their words:
Why do you need the priority seat?
There's nothing really wrong with your feet —

How guilty do you feel, they want to know
For choosing to have kids even though
They've had to see you in *this sort of state*
Burdening them with *such emotional weight*

They praise your partner for his *bravery to stay*
Then seemed shocked at the anger you display
Strangers demand to know exactly what's wrong
And then they're offended if you don't play along

Stories are demanded in the most unexpected places
Buses, toilets, changing rooms and 'safe' internet spaces
Please justify your existence while we wait for the tram
Most stop only just short of an actual physical exam

What they can see never quite seems to be enough
And the invisible stuff, they decide, must be just a bluff
They say I'm too young at first, and then, I should be *flattered*
Because really, if it's all true, I'd look way more battered

The pink hair is just about covering a cracked-up cranium
And thankfully you can't see the clips of pure titanium
Holding together the bits of brain that already tried but failed
To off me in an instant but thankfully I prevailed

Pick your jaw up off the floor when I say I've got a job
Those stereotypical assumptions mark you out as a snob
Drop that head tilt and that patronising *oh, hun...*
In fact, stop speaking, this conversation's done

FRAGILE

They pronounced my bones imperfect from the start
Defective Type 1 collagen plays a big part
My eyes are blue but not in the right place
Spacing slightly off, kids call me 'Alien Face'
Teachers warn classmates to be careful as I could break
So they hit, pinch and punch and then call me a fake
'Til one trips me outside and I land on my arm, hard
I roll slowly on to my back so they can all regard
The compound fracture and its associated gore
Bone ripping through skin and blood on the floor
The Trunchbull dinner-lady's abuse dies on her lips
The hand reaching to yank me up is back firmly on her hips
Her face drains of colour except for a hint of green
Her skin takes on a somewhat cold and slightly sweaty sheen
She barks at the owner of the tripping leg to go for help
Shock is fading now and the pain is making me yelp
I'm also partly fascinated; I can actually *see* the bone
Normally confined to x-rays where the nasty breaks are shown
An ambulance is coming, and I've caused quite a stir
All's well and good but my vision starts to blur
The pain is now roaring and I feel distinctly sick
I can hear the sirens; they've arrived pretty quick
Surveying my tormentors — none will meet my eye
A particularly shitty one is having a wee cry
A tiny little bit of me actually feels quite triumphantly proud
For far too long their taunting has left me so cowed
Now I've been proven legit — and in spectacular style
They really weren't lying when they said I was fragile

GET THE STUDENTS IN

We'd like to get the students in if you don't mind?
Of course, we'll understand if you decide to decline
It's just — you're such a good one for us to test them out
There's not so many of you OIs about
And the brain haemhorrage stuff will stump them for certain
Don't give them any clues; I'll be right behind the curtain

You can tell them the birth tales if they decide to ask
But you're not in labour now, so that won't count as a failed task
They'll maybe get the fibro if they remember to check your meds
That type of ataxia, though, will go right over their heads
Hearing-wise, you can throw them a bone if you wish —

Then they dramatically draw back the curtain with a swish...

Here is your patient; have a poke, use your eyes
Really, she is very basic — straightforward, no lies
Or nasty surprises; nothing rare or too hidden
Remember, though, asking for her help is forbidden
She understands that you all have to learn
So she'll wait patiently until you've all taken a turn

They peer and they prod me, curiosity naked
Fingers pull up eyelids, basic information is stated
Pulse is timed, pressure taken and arms extended out
One looks at my feet and excitedly proclaims it's gout —
The doctor rolls his eyes and the class quickly copies
Good grief! He exclaims. That really is quite sloppy!

Chastened, the student redoubles his effort
Moving around me quickly in his haste to show merit:
Conjunctivitis! He pronounces, sounding quite certain
The doctor makes him go and stand outside the curtain

He seems quite deflated that no-one has yet deduced
Anything at all from this fascinating patient he produced
Bored with them now, he instead recites the medical list
Then smiles as they squirm at all the things that they missed
Quickly, now, the questions on my head begin to pile

This time, like always, I will be here for a while

SEARCHING FOR LABELS

Searching for labels
That are accurate and fit
Some are theoretically correct
But still make me feel like shit

Brittle-bones disease, for one
Sounds like something I could transmit
Being bisexual took me decades
To feel able to admit

Dyslexia? I ventured
No, you're lazy and should quit —
Looking for excuses
You should just get on with it

I never wanted to be called 'abused'
But it was confirmed each time I was hit
And isolated from the world
As to my room I was sent to sit

After taking a parent to court
I'd sift through the writ
Wondering if this made those labels thrown at me
Any more legit

From comments and responses
My mind starts to knit
A distorted-blanket-body-image
And to my memory I commit

Some of them fit nicely
I revel in Northern grit
Cheerfully accept compliments
About accompanying bone-dry wit

Others felt like acid was
Spit straight into my eyes
Words and image distorted:
Could I just omit these lies?

Eventually I learned
Labels didn't always stick
With the ones I had accepted
I could bare to simply sit

Redefine their meanings
Until I felt I could acquit
Myself and behave congruently in line
With my own personal remit

NAMES

My name is Fiona
I am the cis woman you see
I have preferred pronouns
Which are *her* and *she*

Working-class Northerner
Was bestowed on me at birth
Then I was beaten with it regularly,
Told it meant I had no worth

Disabled is a label
I first got at the age of three
It took my brother breaking
For them to figure what was wrong with me

Family labels are funny ones;
They are simply bestowed
Titles come with expectations
And assumed debts that are owed

Graduate is one
That left me feeling besieged
It also meant a heap of debt
After promising prestige

I knew who I was attracted to
Tried to ignore the fact I was bi
Plus did it really matter since
I decided to marry a guy?

Mother was one I chose
With hope but also fear
Of repeating past mistakes
As well as turning into a sphere

Survivor was one it took me
A very long time to claim
To shake of self-recriminations
Of trauma, guilt and shame

Now, *pensioner* was a shock
Awarded at the age of thirty-two
Medically retired already?
But I had so much left to do...

Brain-damaged remains conflicting
Whether or not to share
I know there's plenty of assumptions
And prejudice, and rebuttals to prepare

Psychotherapist was a label I worked for
Having been in the other chair
Survived good and bad support
And felt I had something valuable to share

Music writer was one I created
In my bedroom on my own
I wrote about what I listened to
Not have done the degree first if I'd known

All of these titles are valid, but are still
Labels, like outfits that I wear
Names bestowed and chosen
Whether or not they should be there

When they're all removed and I'm
Left naked, future still unknown
I am still secure and certain
Of the true name which is my own.

INVISIBLE

It's odd to exist
But be mostly unseen
Now you're part of group
Coalesced into a routine
The hospital gives you a number
The DWP do the same
Now nobody notices you
Unless they want someone to blame

Your name becomes irrelevant
As into boxes you are folded
Try to explain the conditions inside
And many will be revolted
So they look above you
As if you're not really there
Talk over, under and for you
Quickly becoming unaware

It's not always done on purpose
Not a deliberate choice to ignore
Some people accidentally forget you
You can't do as much as you could before:
Without quite ever realising
You find yourself adrift
And when you get pulled up —
Disappearance can be swift

SPLIT THE BILL

You spring the idea that we could *split the bill* —
I smile, scream internally, and pray my debit card will
Stretch to cover the booze you drank alongside all three courses
While I had as little as I could. Your assumption reinforces
The invisibility I feel as The Poorer Friend
The one who has no more credit left to bend
You always complain if you don't get to see me
But never choose the option of stuff I can do freely
Sitting in the park or coming 'round to mine
The implied option to spare my pocket you decline
Instead you spring meals, presents and travel
Seemingly unaware of the frantic battle
Your careless suggestions unleash in my mind
Calculating yet more energy and money I've got to find
Periodically you cock your head to the side — poor you —
Oh, and all that *horrible* stuff you have been through
I grit my teeth but hope this might finally be the time
The difference in our circumstances might start to chime
I don't want your pity, or even worse, your charity
I just want you to realise what I mean by austerity
It's not your guilt I'm trying to trip — honestly, I swear
But please — give me some sign that you actually care
Please stop putting me in situations where I have to chose
Whether it's my dignity or next week's food money I have to lose
I don't weigh my relationships using pounds and pence
Nor do I assign depth of love to the level of expense
Nor do I ascribe intent directly to the level of cash
Communicate importance with the amount that I splash
I am not begging or parading poverty for tips
I'm honestly happy with just a bowl of chips
Just don't put me under this obligation anymore
And maybe some find cheaper options to explore

MUSIC NERD

Blasting music loudly enough to envelop my brain
Fine-tuning my mood along with the equalisers
Sliding one euphoric dance mix into the next; keep the dopamine-
tingling-lift
Slamming angry rock into angsty indie sliced with punk fury
Spliced with MTV idents stolen direct to my boombox
Two-Tone to wrap up political polemic for me to pogo to
Songs to play on an internal loop during medical procedures
Anthems worthy of being entrance music into a boxing ring
Disco for rising up from the depths of despair
Industrial and synth as an ever-present heartbeat
Eurotrash mixed with pop-tastic hits to heal heartbreak
Peppered through songs to take you right back to a dark moment
Skip the track and blink back into the present
Songs to elicit the kick inside to educate baby before it's even born
Excruciating pain forgotten in a mosh pit or hanging off a barrier
Jumping up and down knowing the price I'd pay for it
And not caring
Making the world shut its mouth while I yelled in its face
Like a church where you sing the hymns back to God
No need to have faith because the miracle is one you can touch
Neck tingling, hands in the air waiting for the drop

People see it as part of who you are
The person ready with a lyric
With a lot of random trivia at her fingertips
Who has always heard of that song you thought only you liked
That one that has read the book, seen the video

Has a song or five for any situation you care to conjure up
Whether asked to provide one or not
This ever-present, expertly curated cacophony following every
moment large and small
Playing endlessly
Muffling life to ease reality

Until

One of the biggest moments occurred with no sound
Just a sudden, silent explosion
Suddenly drowning in blood
It washed everything away
And stole all the music from me
Brutal, echoing silence

A brain so broken and bruised it rejected all sound and song
A pain I wasn't used to; one with no reprieve
Gifted so many albums I can't play
Given with love, fear and crippling impotency
This is how we know you, they say
We don't know what else to do

A vacuum allowing the screams to morph into music
To shatter everything, unopposed
Lost suddenly in a wide-open space
No soundtrack to focus on or absorb fear
No map to navigate this land of confusion
No hair and no headphones
No constant companion and touchstone
No idea if I'll see tomorrow
The silver girl sailed without me and no one can scoop me up

Adrift in silence
Can't even count on the endless lyrics others knowingly or not
quote to press the play button
But you're alive, they say
Be glad for that, they say
I am, I say

But I've lost something that's more intrinsic than I can explain
Even if aphasia wasn't robbing me of the ability to be understood

No mixtape to create and explain for me
There's a song or a lyric or a word for this somewhere
But for me, they've all gone
Playlist corrupted
Mixtape chewed up and   spat out

So

Tentatively trying to start again
Trying to soothe a migraine of many months with soft sweet
balms
Whispers of tunes played so low
Sotto soul singing me back sweetly
From despair to where now?

Building up a tolerance
                    slowly

The fear of moving my head at all eventually giving way
To the irresistible urge to mark the beat with my body somehow
Clocks, brain scans, the tram door clicks start the metronome
Quietly, slowly hope flickers into a flame that all is not lost
These are not the days when the music dies

The encyclopaedia you owned has warped
 and ripped yes
At least the music is still loose inside your head
I can still hear music
This sequel does have a soundtrack
The band will play on
Until the hourglass has no more grains of sand

THEY SAY THEY WERE POOR TOO

But look at you gone out when you talk about getting your winter
coat from the social in town
Leopold Square. Sounds posh
They never trudged into a formerly-grand place now housing a
display of benevolence to the poor
They never queued up to wait their turn

Were never eyed-up quickly, size determined and handed the
girls' or boys' coat without a word
Never experienced the uncomfortable stares and hostile mouths
When you ask if you can have a boys' coat too
Please, because
You don't really wear girls clothes

You try to explain that
Pink makes you feel conspicuous
The bands of muted black and blue separated with a tiny seam of
red of the boys' coat makes fading into the background much
easier
Trousers have already proved safer than skirts
Wandering hands have to fight harder to get their goal when
there's more fabric to negotiate
It gives you longer to try and escape
But you just say *please* and also *sorry* but
Could you have the boys' shoes too?
The girls' ones pinch your feet and rub you raw
You're honestly not trying to be difficult; you really are grateful
that your betters deem you pathetic enough to need free clothes
once a year
Thank you no really, you weren't dragged up
You had manners beaten into you
It's just that...

You're going to get the shit kicked out of you again next week at school
When your new coat and shoes single you and the other scrubbers out as poor
Your free-school-meal pass will be used against you
The lack of known labels and obvious hand me downs weaponised in the playground
So you don't need the colour of the coat to make you even more of a target
You do need the shoes to be less crippling so you have a chance of running away
And you pray to God you won't grow again like you did last time.
Six weeks into new shoes and they no longer fit
You have no choice but to get on with it

But they never got their winter coat from the social

And a decade later, NHS specs are in
And poor is declared Britpop-cool
And you don't understand how the same people who spat at you
And hit you
And ridiculed your clothes
Now embrace charity-shop-chic, proudly claim their own lowly beginnings
But they had homes with food and heat and holidays in places you couldn't pronounce
Brought actual money in to buy their lunch and sweets at break time
They always smelled and looked clean while you just felt ashamed

They didn't get their winter coat from the social

Now old becomes *vintage* and jumble sale is *totes a vibe*
And you are priced out. All you're left with is cheap, fast-fashion

Which becomes another stick to beat you with
Yes you know it won't last and it's not good for the planet
But you still don't have the luxury of choice
It's this or racking up more debt on your catalogue account
Always paying much more than it's worth
And that's before they add the sky-high interest that buying stuff on tick always brings

They never got their winter coat from Primark.
You can't get them from the social any more.

Still, at least your poor uniform is much more varied these days
Now we are adults we don't quite know what to do
You might manage to wing it and pass
Some of them like to adopt a poor person to make themselves look better
So I guess you might get to be someone's pet
They say you should be yourself and no-one judges the poor any more
Fuck the Tories and *down with that sort of thing*
But if you take the risk and tell the truth
The result is confusing
Some might still reject you but of those that don't
Many say they were poor too

But look at you gone out when you talk about getting your winter coat from the social

BOOKS

My family say I have far too many books
When another box arrives I see them exchange looks
But equally they understand the spells the book weave
Never more so than when my bed I can't leave
They are soothing, too, at the end of the day
When I've no energy left, given it all away

Stories saved me when little, confused and lonely
Anne imagined with me that we could be less homely
George was a girl but had a boy's name
No-one bossed her or made hitting her the game
Jo March and I could both be quite stubborn
Our anger and tears we both struggled to govern

The Bible was full of stories I was told to study
Lots seemed graphic and also quite bloody
Daniel was rather unfairly sent into the lion's den
Jonah and Job were another two unlucky men
Even Christ knows, when He finally arrives
He will not be getting out of this place alive

Finally, the freedom to read the books I chose
So many tales to explore in poetry and prose
Many more lives than I would ever live
All with experience and knowledge to give
Guides to accompany me on what I went through
Or prepare me as a new challenge swam into view

Edwyn gave me hope that I could recover and laugh again
Betty educated and invited me into her wicked sexy den
Lovelace introduced me to a new galaxy of stars
Anthony exposed and detailed all his scars
Emily shared her monsters worries with me
Julia convinced me to be out, bi and free

The many musicians whose tales light up my head
Especially when I'm lying down, unable to leave my bed
History, culture, scandal and death
Society, psychology, kink and I hold my breath
As I take down another bundle of words from the bookcase
Open the cover to journey on to the next place

YELLOW STICKER

Travelling down the conveyor belt
Packaged and shipped and arrived and opened and inspected
They decided which aisle to put you on
Displayed prominently with a special promotion:
Finest? Standard? Value brand?
Pick the price point to label a life
Keep it fresh
Serving suggestions:
Long-life or short-dated?
Lots of information printed on the packaging
That can't be removed
But can be covered up with sale stickers
Top deal! Two for one!
Even cheaper with your store card!
The stickers are bright and cheerful
But start to curl up on the edges the longer you sit on the shelf
Left behind as the products around you are snapped up
Finally they come to gather you up too
But not into a basket
No sense of purpose restored and expectations rewarded
This is it; Last Shelf Saloon
Now the stickers are yellow
Not like sunshine or daffodils
But warning sign yellow, toxic and sickly
They knock your price down again
Chipping off your value more as the final date approaches
Reduced, removed and finally recycled
Deemed entirely worthless
Swept with one arm into a bin
Banished and forgotten forever

Somewhere on the conveyor belt a new product line is being
labelled

LIVING EULOGY

So this is what it's like then,
Being at your own funeral.
Not quite haunting the lectern
Or making the entry music skip:
We've not got as far as the crem
No-one is sitting tearfully in the pews
But these Facebook feeds and Twitter threads
They read like a eulogy all the same.
Terse updates read *is it serious?*
I didn't know
Then
They have to do brain surgery as soon as possible

Will she be OK?

She could die. She can't die. I don't know how to be without her.
Then
They've taken her to surgery. Now we wait.
And
I don't know what to say to our children

If we can do anything let us know

Then
She's out and alive but we don't know much else.

They've moved her to HDU now.

Under every update, the conversation flows
Comfort, encouragement and optimism offered to try and soothe
She will be OK. We all know how stubborn she is.
Then the eulogy starts.
Slowly at first:
If you wanted my attention, Fish, you didn't have to go to extremes...
    I meant to message her to arrange a meet up. Why didn't I sort that?
I keep looking at the last thing she posted, it was only a few minutes
before it happened. It feels so weird.

I keep refreshing. Hoping for more news.

Kiss From a Rose came on the radio and I started laughing; do you
remember that time...

There is a brief pile-on of laughing and karaoke horror stories
There is the odd threat too
I'm going to kill you young lady for scaring the shit out of me
Quickly starts to flow into
Profile pictures changing to different memories
And
Oh god do you remember when she...
Songs start to haunt people but in a nice way
I just played One Step Beyond and thought of you
Photos of parties and messy nights out are shared
Memories are swapped
I've been thinking a lot about this time she and I....
              I found this mixtape she made me over a decade ago
Will they let the kids see her yet?
                      Oh God, please wake up

Moods are momentarily lifted
She's doing a bit better. She can't really talk yet, but smiled
Then
They don't seem very happy, I don't know what's happening.
              Stay hopeful, we all have to stay hopeful
She's trying to talk but the aphasia means she is making no sense
Until
She says hi. She's feeling a bit shit
Notifications explode
Master of understatement as ever then
                    Oh my god she is talking?
Who needs a lift and who is visiting when?
A photo of a half-shaven, stapled-together head with a woozy
smile is posted
Blue thumbs, red hearts and yellow smiles rack up
The eulogy is nearly done

Plans are starting to be made
Tentatively but with hope

We still have to get to 4 weeks to pass the immediate danger zone
    They keep asking her who the Prime Minister is; she's not happy about
                                                                    that.
They snuck the kids on to the other ward so she's seen them!
                                        They just held each other
A wake for a woman who's finally actually awake
                                        ends.

It's strange seeing what everyone writes when they think you
might not make it
The memories and stories they share to pass time while they wait
(Some of which you're glad they heavily edited for a public
audience)
The encouragement and hope offered
Because there is always hope
Until there isn't
Floating, haunting your own nearly-funeral
Hearing the conversations and paying attention
Noting that no-one is talking about those things you spent so long
and so much effort trying to hide or change
Even the embarrassing stories are spun with affection not derision
That the people who love you, love all of you, including the bits
you hate

KNOW YOUR PLACE

Born with a womb
So required to procreate
In specific circumstances only:
In a sanctified union
Produce more servants
For an unseen God

Meet everyone else's needs
Have none of your own
Conform to gendered expectations
Told so many times
This is the role for a woman
To serve without the question
Love without malice
Belong to one man
Then be given to another

A contract formed above your head
Sealing your body and mind
Into a new life of service
Reproduce effortlessly and quietly
As long as you don't sin
All will go to plan
Pop out babies like peas from a pod
Efficiently
Healthily

Raise and praise boys
Form girls into obedient wives for the next generation
Sexuality is sinful if it's not straight
Either way — to enjoy sex is unseemly
Don't have an opinion. Or, worse — a personality
Be intelligent but not more than a man
Women, you must know your place
Or face the consequences:

What were you wearing?
Did you give him a come-on?
Subjugate all you want for others
No questions to be asked or answered
Blind faith is demanded and expected
It's gods way
It's the right way
It's the only way
Be small, delicate and demure
Eat — but not too much
Exercise strict self-control
Dress modestly

Most of all
Be quiet
Shut up
Don't cry

Laugh occasionally but briefly
Your laugh should tinkle
Not snort, or make your belly jiggle
Or your eyes water
A woman should be invisible unless needed
Gliding effortlessly around in the background
Completing chores with no expectation of praise
A ghost running the machine:
A house, a husband and a family

And I thought
Fuck this

MARRIAGE

From watching my parents, I thought marriage was a struggle
Two people locked in some strange tussle
No affection; no connection
One needing the other to cook and serve
The other needing spiders summarily squashing
It was using the same anniversary card every year
Mini-earthquakes causing fault lines which widen
One can't see the ground is disappearing until they're in
free

fall
The other then abandoned trying to patch the fissure
Stepping away into the secret arms of another
Court papers and recriminations
Abandonment and mental disintegration
Children left trying to hold parents lives together

Coming from that, you'd perhaps be surprised to hear that
    marriage still felt a necessity to me, when I was a child
A form of safety
Even though I could see how wrong it could go
At one point it still seemed the only event that might offer me a
    kind-of freedom
Until a legal union with a 30 year-old man was suggested
    for 13 year-old me
Worse, he seemed as keen as our fathers did
Running was the only option
So I ran —
Straight into immature, lying arms at age 16
Saying no to that offer never seeming like an option
So I said yes —
Two years later I said I was jilted;
What I meant was **freed**
So why run down the aisle nine years later?
Holding hands and giggling

In a red dress to a nutty love song
One baby heckling from the front row
Another preparing their first kick in-utero
No nerves and (possibly) minimal respect for this legal process
Albeit one with posh clothes and place settings
New rings exchanged to replace ones we'd worn for years
Practical considerations unromantically playing their part
As you nearly died, we should lodge the paperwork, just in case...
Sign and seal something already firmly in existence
A reason to lose a name weighted with pain and
Take one shared with new humans we made
Not given away by anyone to anyone
Walking forward together, like we always had

Why, though?
Why engage in an age old custom steeped in patriarchal bullshit?
Rejecting any vow that demand I obey
Because we both knew no two marriages are the same
We could continue to build us in whatever way we wanted
Names could change — and social prefixes too if we chose
Roles with enshrined names like husband or wife
Didn't have to be taken on if we didn't want to bear that weight
No expectations or obligations suddenly brought into existence
    because we said words laid down in law

We practiced our vows but forget the words now
The meaning we gave them remains crystal clear
We play at being adults but not at being responsible
Wifey and Hubby: terms leading to immediate divorce
Anniversaries an excuse to take archaic traditions and spin
 them into unexpected gifts
Time and attention we try to gift **all** year around
Those humans we made are nearly fully grown and thinking
 about flying the crowded, tumbledown nest we cobbled
 together

And occasionally fix with tape, string and hope
Quite often they tell us off
Comments and innuendos they've finally figured out
They catch us hugging
One smiles at us from a distance
Comfortable that way
The other forces themselves into the warm space between us
Glories in heat, touch & familiar smells
Both firmly rooted as they increasingly grow in their own ways
As it always was I hope it always will be

Mixtapes will always be made
Passing years marvelled at
Catastrophes will be handled and hope held
Sometimes decisions and mistakes will stretch us to our limits
But those strains will remain acknowledged and worked on
Our autonomous lives remain happily, deliberately tangled
Independent where desired as well
Need for the other stretching far beyond the provision of dinner
or dispatching of arachnoids
Of flouncy dresses and speeches
Gains and goals met are celebrated not a source of insecurity to
throw at each other
A future unwritten but consciously chosen

PARENT

When we decided to try and have children,
We knew nothing could be assumed for certain
Or that we'd suddenly be pulled behind
My body's own privacy curtain

Everything inside minutely examined
Labelled and laid out starkly
Each possible devastation
Intricately drawn out, sharply

Body parts and motivations
Measured and endlessly tested
More scans and more appointments
Insistently suggested

But no-one really talked
About what it would be like to make a child
Making another actual human being
Was an idea we still found pretty wild

While everyone seemed focused
On anything that could go wrong
We were also focused on how the
Baby seemed to react to a song

On the craving for food I'd never liked
Or the way the person we made might be
Eyes, hair colour, chin and nose
What would come from him and what from me?

There were names to be selected
So many accessories which were all brand new
Grappling with equipment on precisely no sleep
Unknown skills learned, tests we'd be put through

Work would be hard
We know money would be tight
Plus figuring out childcare
Which simply had to be right

Then to a death defying labour
(Would you really expect anything less?)
But we both made it
With the requisite amount of mess

So then we were a family
With a box fresh human we couldn't break
Taking the risk to make another one
Was a calculation we were prepared to make

So then we had got two and
Debated adding one more kid
Then my brain exploded and they said
Of your womb we have to get rid

We can't get you through
Another pregnancy safely
Any further baby would have to be aborted
They added, gravely

So I gave up my fertility
To protect the children I already had
First, glorified paper-clips bunged in my tubes
Didn't seem quite so bad

Later the whole factory
Was condemned and had to go
The interior was already trashed
Even if outside it didn't really show

Premature menopause chased me
To be fair I didn't run that far
Bring on the mid-life crisis
Get me an electric guitar

Endless moments that didn't
Make into your milestone book
You lived them though them too
Sometimes I catch it in a look

Tiny fragile seedlings now
Almost fully grown
It won't be too much longer before
Away from home you've flown

Through joy or tears
One thing was always apparent
All of it was worth it
Because it made me your parent

BLATANTLY BISEXUAL

Hello world: let me enunciate clearly
The way I fancy people is patently queery
Like delicate petals starting to unfurl
I realise it's not just boys, but also girls

Joyfully I realise this goes beyond the binary
But all around me, others are derisory
Homophobic hate pours into my ears
My authenticity smothered by other people's fears

Apparently to be different is unnatural
God's word on the matter is apparently unilateral
It's incredible my brains capacity to deny
That I'd ever fancied anyone who wasn't a guy

That there's something different about girl crushes
Differentiating desperately to spare my blushes
Joking they'd be the one if I was going to turn
Trying to ignore that shameful lying burn

Forcing myself to forget kisses and touches
Got to protect myself from Satan's clutches
Telling myself it's somehow intellectual
When I'm actually blatantly bisexual

Passing off girlfriends by dropping a syllable
Trying to make the feelings shared more permissible
Scared of rejection and being called perverted
By god, friends and family I will be deserted

It was when my children cheerfully came out
Calmly sure that the only thing I'd care about
Was them feeling who they were was accepted
That their pronouns and identities would always be respected

But I was being crushed by incredible weight
That increased every time I said I was straight
They told me I could come out too
What you said to us, we say to you

Validity is yours for you to claim
You don't have to carry anyone else's shame
How you define your identity is your choice
No one ever gets to silence your voice

MADE OF STERN STUFF

Made of stern stuff they say
Real Northern grit
But at least tha's never actually been
Sent down the pit

Still I feel my bones
Often splinter and crumble
Explosions and rescues
Leave nerve endings all jumbled

I work so hard not to let my face
Betray the reality of pain
Trying to behave as if
Everything still just the same

That my head is not
A burning scarred lumpy mess
Hair dyed obnoxiously bright pink
To hide that there is less

Swallowing screams and smiling
Suffocating any rouge sobs
Finding a soothing rhythm instead
In different types of jobs

Until it overwhelms me
The terrible two lay me out
Chronic pain and fatigue
To their cause so devout

I no longer try to fight them
This body is a lost cause
But medication and wilfulness are
Still enough to make them pause

Music to set a rhythm so I can
Match pain to the beat
Often makes it easier
To remain just about on my feet

Acceptance not defeat
Cushions the inescapable known
These conditions are degenerative
Eventually they'll get me alone

Decay is inevitable
The price of the privilege to age
And in many ways the reality
Keeps me in pains cage

But in other ways I'm freer
Than I've ever really been
No longer trying to pass as able
Not frightened of being seen

You might get it, or not
Either options fine
These days I'm much more confident
In keeping my own time

I medicate my body with
An assortment of coloured pills
Patches, creams even zapping
Muscles with tenns techno thrills

Food so carefully managed
Scans, scopes and x-rays
And let's be honest, hospital takes up
Most of my allotted holidays

Still, tha's made of stern stuff they say
Proper Sheffield woman of steel
Not quite, I wish internally
But yes, I am the real deal

ATTENTION

I promise you that I really am trying to pay attention
But my focus doesn't fit in with the ideals of convention
It's not deliberately rude but I do get distracted
And then I realise that our conversation's being impacted
It's not that you're boring, not in the slightest
But that idea you sparked feels like the brightest
Light filling up all of my brain
And all other thoughts just got flushed down the drain

Now you're looking expectantly waiting for me to respond
I'm trying to track back to a place now beyond
My brain's ability to recall and hold in a firm grip
What was it you were saying when my focus started to slip?
Maybe it was about your job, where is it you work?
I'm hoping it's safe to assume someone there's a jerk?
Trying to rely on making noises to get back into the flow
Also looking for an acceptable reason I need to go

Rest my head against the door in the toilet stall
Berate myself for all the names and facts I can't recall
I resist the urge to hit my head, I know it's doing its best
But I still choke on all the things knotted, unspoken in my chest
Cringe at the memories of conversations I interrupted with thought
Song lyrics and observations that had not been sought
I try to will my mouth to stay shut but none of me will behave
My brain signals I'm drowning but my mouth just sees me wave

On the other hand music gives me a dopamine tingle
Ideas that spark off each other, masterplans seem so simple
A treasury of collected facts, snippets of information held
An appetite for finding out more that will not be quelled
Creativity and curiosity with laser focus on one place
At least for now, we know I can't avoid the eventual fate
Another hobby, impulse buy shoved under the bed
Until the next thing reignites the fire in my head

SPARE THE ROD

Spare the rod, spoil the child it was said —
So the rod was not spared
Nor the open palm or closed fist
The belt strap or the buckled end
Nails cut sharp straight across
Leave scratches to border each finger print

The threat I won't be able to sit down
For a month of Sundays
Though a month of any day would surely last as long?
Fear and shame though, eventually gives way to ambivalence
Knowing there will always be punishment meted out for some
                                        misdemeanour
Some I know will warrant a beating
Talking too much or sticking my elbows out when eating
Rope is tied around the offending joints still won't clip my
wings enough
Asking to go to the toilet is wrong
Saying I'm hungry is bad
Falling asleep during a 3-hour long prayer is unforgivable

Other crimes are only apparent in the committing of the offence
Answer too many questions on Blockbusters
Slipping and breaking a bone
Wearing clothes that are too skimpy — when it's all you have
Being tired
Being confused

Teachers know but decide not to see
Dirty clothes and unwashed body
Bruises in the changing room seen
Exhaustedly trying not to fall asleep mid-lesson
A couple give you kind eyes but are silent when you try to speak
Childline confirms it's abuse but you hang up.
It's a label you can't take.

Besides, maybe it was the rod that spoilt the child
Absconding to play with a friend is wrong yes
But at least the next beating would be earned for doing
something fun
Now this rebellious fever is growing not shrinking
If being a good girl won't stop the punishment, why even try?
Following the ever-changing rules will still somehow be wrong
after all
Breaking them at least makes the next eruption less of a surprise
The promise of violence is neutering any fear
Resignation doesn't lessen the pain but the adrenaline has cashed
out
No more spikes or swings
Pulling a fridge apart with your bare hand in front of me
Smash your plates at my feet
I know I'll be next, because I always am
Until I'm not

Walking away in just what I'm wearing
Freezing in a blazing summer heat
Fourteen, just — but free

BUT I'M NOT MIDDLE CLASS

They say I stopped being working class
When I picked up my degree
They said, *You're middle class, actually,*
But I don't agree

Intelligence was never
Class's defining trait
Miners **do** read Dickens
Steelworkers understood their fate

I grew up around music
And books bought for pence
Living in a fantasy world
In that context, made sense

I consumed food with my eyes
I knew I'd never get to eat
Ran with heroes, adding their wings
To my own broken feet

Fighting to hold on to an education
Others wanted to deny
Said I wanted to go to Uni
Advised not to aim so high

A YTS might be a more achievable goal,
They suggest
Stubbornly, I reply, 'I will, somehow,
Pass every single test.'

Surviving university but
Drowning in unfathomable debt
Holding on by my finger-tips
No changing class just yet

So while I don the cap and
Struggle into the gown
Smile for photos, poverty
Still holds me firmly down

I didn't get the magic jobs that paid well
Were in any way secure
Instead working in conditions
That were hard to endure

Cleaning up bodily fluids
Endless hours to pay the rent
Come pay day though
The moneys already been spent

No family to rely on with money
To come to my aid
Cold, hungry, poverty
Promised success begins to fade

Working class to me means
Accepting often having very little
Any sense of ease and comfort
Always feeling brittle

But it also means other things
Often a community with bonds
Neighbours, sometimes strangers,
In difficult times respond

Dignity in where we come from
That *where there's muck, there's brass*
An expectation to contribute
No-one gets a free pass

That skills are as valid as
Figures in a bank account
You are not your salary
Considered paramount

Less time for social niceties
Blunter, that's true
But also much less pretense:
It'll be seen straight through

Food that's cheap but filling
Pies that stick to your ribs
Quick-off, draw for the Yorkies
Before someone else calls dibs

We work and know that no-one else
Will be there to pick up the bill
Making ends meet
Is a lifelong, unseen skill

Making fuel from the cruel
Inaccurate stereotypes
So I will continue to proudly wear
My working-class stripes

ELOCUTE THIS

You might have heard this story
I feel like I tell it to everyone
Because spinning being shamed
Into something that feels more fun

Sort-of takes the sting
From the memory of being told
The way I talk is wrong —
If therapy is going to be sold

Clients will expect more —
If you want them to actually pay
They'll expect a level of intelligence
That's not apparent you have when you say

Nah then, thee, or *Hendos*
or call somebody *love*
But if you learn to speak proper
They'll think you're a cut above

Ge'ore I think to mysen
I sound like I come from Sheffield!
Although true others do seem shocked
When me birthplace is revealed

They say I sound too posh
Tha's never lived on't Manor! They sneer —
But I have — and several other postcodes too —
And I do sound like I come from round 'ere.

Others make incorrect assumptions
When they hear I live in Grimesthorpe
Oooh, look at all your silly stereotypes
I am starting to bend and warp

Does my accent get broader
The further I go down south?
Of course it does, comparatively, but
It's always Northern what comes out me mouth

I never took elocution lessons
Couldn't afford them for a start
And even then I knew being me was reyt
I didn't need to play a part

I qualified for the record
And no one's ever refused to pay
It matters to them *what* — not *how* —
I say what I need to say

ACKNOWLEDGEMENTS

To Chris and Lin for patiently listening to eighteen (on average) great new plans a week (each) and never once saying any of them were impossible. Impractical on occasion, yes, but never impossible. And for being there before and after every surgery and through every recovery.

To all my friends in all the different groups and places, family especially the family I found and made; thank you for never giving up on me.

To Rebecca Kenny and Written Off for putting something excellent out into the world that I somehow managed to find. I'd not restarted writing poetry very long before I found you on Instagram and within weeks was reading a poem to a room full of people for the first time ever. That will always be a special memory.

And to Freddie Mercury, Henderson's Relish, Marian Keyes, Suggs, Nick Hornby, Tori Amos, my original boombox, Sheffield and all the other musicians, writers and the city that shaped and inspire me.

ABOUT THE AUTHOR

Photo: © Ary Hutchings

Fiona Hutchings is a poet, parent and nerd with too many books, music records and medical conditions to keep track of. She writes about her experiences of disability, fractured family and fractured bones. As well as the rare congenital degenerative bone disease she was born with, Fiona has collected various other medical diagnosis over the years. She has survived one brain haemorrhage which nearly killed her, two brain surgeries and is really hoping these things don't come in threes.

She started writing in childhood and made her TV debut reading a poem on Jackanory's 25th Anniversary programme. It was about a woman catching the same X55 bus home with her one evening whose tragic demeanour caught her eye. Fiona took a break from poetry to have two children, retrain as a therapist and defy death a few times. She has been a music journalist for online magazine Penny Black Music since 2009 and works with young people and adults as a psychotherapist.

ABOUT THE PUBLISHER

It started with a key.

Written Off is a publishing company founded in and run from the North of England. Its logo, a bent and non-functional key, is based on the bent front-door key that Rebecca Kenny found in her pocket after arriving home from hospital following her car crash. It is a symbol of change, new starts, risk and taking a chance on the unknown.

Having her car written off, her career written off, and then being somewhat written off herself, Rebecca chose the company's name with an aim to reclaim power from adversity and show that just because society maintains a status quo, that doesn't mean you can't make waves.

Written Off do not charge for submissions, we do not charge to publish and we make space for writers who may struggle to access traditional publishing houses, specifically writers who are neuro-divergent or otherwise marginalised. We never ask anyone to write for free, and we like to champion authentic voices.

All of our beautiful covers are designed by our graphic designer Sam at SMASH Designs, a graphic design company based in Southport, Merseyside.

Find us online at writtenoffpublishing.com